5 IRONS DON'T FLO

(Dealing with Anger on the Golf Course)

by

Andrew Dunkley

Copyright © 2016

(Warning: contains offensive language)

Language

Just so you know, this book is about golf...more
to the point it's about one of the worst things
a golfer faces, ANGER. So be warned it does
contain "course" language. Yes, a pun was
intended there because most of the expletives
I'm talking about happen on the golf course
during play and if you're reading this you know
exactly what I mean.

"Fuuuuuuuuuuuuuuuuuuuuuuuuuuuuuuck!"

Yes, that word echoes across golf courses all
too often. And I'm sure you've heard the old
adage. Why do we use the word golf? Because
fuck was already taken.

But it's not just about bad language, it's also

about tantrums, losing your shit and destroying any chance of playing a decent game. Worse still you may be one of those who carry a bad round for hours or even days. I've been there too.

Now I don't intend to drag this out. This will be a short book because I know golfers don't like to do much reading, even on greens but as a former club captain I know that most of you have never read the 'local rules' on the back of the card, so I won't burden you with too many pages here.

I'm guessing that if you bought this book for the incredibly low price I put on it, it's because you have a temper issue and self destructive tendencies or perhaps you get frustrated, annoyed or simply lose your cool occasionally.

Or maybe you drop your bundle big time and

make the game horrible for yourself, your partners and the people residing close to the course who have little kids and birds that can mimic the human tongue.

Whatever the reason, I hope I can help, so read on...

By the way, I'm not here to play nice...I just want to make a point and that is, you're only fucking yourself if you can't control your emotions while playing this game. It's really that simple.

About the author

So who is Andrew Dunkley? Well I'm not a sports psychologist or a professional golfer. There are plenty of those and I do believe most of them know what they're talking about but I'm focussing 100% on anger.

I started playing golf at the age of 12, while in high school. For some reason I found the game fascinating despite the fact that all my friends played tennis or football. I didn't come from a sporting family, so I'm not sure where the sporting gene comes from, but it's there and golf was my chosen game.

I played sporadically for years as a junior then as a young adult. When I started working, golf took a back seat until I moved to a new town and met new neighbours who had the golfing bug. I got back into the game big time and began my pursuit of perfection. I, like many, wanted to be great at this game.

Sadly, it was also when I discovered I had a very foul temper on the course. I mean it was horrendous. I threw clubs, swore, broke equipment, swore, walked off, swore, hated the World, swore and brooded over bad games for an entire week, all the while busting to get out there and have another crack the next weekend.

My form would come and go, like yours I suspect, and my early years were dogged with inconsistency and shitty scores. I couldn't break 100 for the life of me.

Then one day, a friend loaned me a book written by Jack Nicklaus. It wasn't a manual on how to grip, line up, swing, chip or putt the ball...it was about thinking. Jack has written dozens of books and sadly, all these years later the exact title escapes me but "The Lesson Tee" might have been it, written in 1972.

I read it cover to cover and it changed my approach to golf forever!

In one short statement he said, if you play off 20, why then try to par every hole? You should be trying to bogie every hole. That one simple idea was all I needed. I took that thought to the course and suddenly everything was different. Over the next eight games I broke 100 every time with a low round of 87, my first sub 90 round. It was amazing and the only thing that I changed was my attitude.

It also got me thinking about thinking. Thinking better on the course and keeping my crap under control. I started researching and reading about sports psychology and why certain people play better than others at all kinds of levels.

Oh, did I mention that I've been a journalist since 1984? Yep, and I've spoken to a lot of sports people during that time, done a lot of research and got to understand why some people are better at sport than the rest and it's not just technical ability.

I interviewed a tennis coach some years ago, who had just been appointed to the Indian Davis Cup squad and he said that if you watch the world number 1 warming up with the world number 500 you wouldn't see any difference in their ability BUT, and here's the clincher, the world number 1 is better because he keeps his shit together more than anyone else when it matters most.

Self belief goes a long way, that's very true and we can't all expect to be world number 1 or even club champion but you can win the battle again yourself and that's all golf is, a game you play within yourself against your own mind and your emotions and, if you're reading this book, most of the time you lose.

So, after years of playing this game at a club level, reading many books on the golfing brain, interviewing sports psychologists and elite athletes added to my time as a board member and club captain, I do believe I have some thoughts to share on this hazardous element of golf known as anger.

Some thoughts on playing the game

Now at this point I do need to include some remarks on technical skill. If you play off a handicap of 25 and you trying to par all 18 holes, you'll never be happy. One thing I've learned about golf is this. The better you get the better you want to be. No-one ever gives up on improving at this game. That's a very positive thing. Sadly, many of us set a very lofty level of expectation and that's where we come unstuck. More on that later.

After doing my research and interviewing many who work in the sports industry about the emotional side of the game, did I get better? Damn right I did. I've won my share of club events, even cracked a championship trophy, broke par a few times and shot a 69 (while off 7) and have run second five times in stroke and match play championship events... but it wasn't easy. It took discipline and hard work and time. And once you get there, you can't stop working. You have to maintain your clarity and control or you will slide back into that world of ranting and raving and shit golf.

That's why I wrote this book...because I reached a great height only to fall, and I fell hard. There were solid reasons for this, many of which I will get to in the following chapters but let me just say it was more about what was happening off the course that messed me up and that's a factor you may not have considered.

Fighting back from that slump was much harder than I expected. I thought, having done it once and knowing what I learned the first time about keeping the anger under control, it would be easy. It wasn't. I let my guard down and it cost me in ways I never anticipated. My slump lasted over three years.

I've been through a lot of golfing shit, as have you I'm sure, but I've learned a few things along the way, which I sincerely believe can help you.

If not, I won't give you your money back. You bought the book, so suck it up and let's get on with it.

This is not a manual on the technical side of the game. It's quite simply designed to open you up to possible reasons for your reactive emotions and to give you ideas that can help... if you allow yourself to change. AND that is the clincher...you have to want to be a better person on the course.

No-one can ever predict what kind of game they're going to have when they arrive on course. Some start well and finish poorly, some have a mid-round slump while others start terribly and pick it up towards the end.

One interesting factor in golf is the "care-free" approach. You see it sometimes when the chips are down; where the player knows all is lost and over the last few holes they suddenly play great. They've given up trying and worrying and the stress has subsided and they play fluid, carefree shots and redeem themselves at the end of the game. That alone should be a clue as to how you should be on the course, all the time. A clear mind if key.

Another observation I made when I was a club captain was the way some players won club events at key moments in their lives. I noticed a direct correlation between excellent scores (often winning scores) straight after a player retired from their non-golf career. This didn't happen just once...it was quite common.

After years of stress and worry about work and life and meeting expectations, the shackles fell away and life became carefree and that was reflected in a much calmer approach to golf and, oddly enough, better scores. Interesting huh?

Obviously that's not the answer to freaking out on the course for most of us, but it does offer a clue as to how the mind works. When there's nothing to worry about in your life, you (should) play better.

The day I won my championship was interesting. At our club the top eight seeds after the first three rounds played in the final groups for the last round. I was seeded 5, so I played ahead of the top four. My wife was at home and was ill that weekend. I'd taken her to the doctor before the third round then went out, at her insistence, to play. She said "If you don't go, you'll always regret it." I'd been playing fairly poorly over the first two rounds but was still in the mix, only about five shots behind thanks to the pressure of the event on everyone. I shot a good round and that got me into the seeded draw. One element that certainly helped me in the third round was the fact that I played at a different tee time and didn't know anyone in my group and it was clear they were all good friends. I maintained exemplary behaviour throughout the round which translated to better concentration and ultimately a great score.

My wife was still unwell that final day and I offered to stay home and again she insisted I go, "What will it achieve sitting around here,

I'm fine. You have nothing to worry about, everything is good in your life…go and play," she said.

It was weird because I felt incredibly calm after that and when I got to the course I was excited. I saw two mates who were also in seeded draws for their respective grades and talked to them before we all teed off. I explained that I'd never made the seeded draw before and didn't know what to expect.

Both had been in final seedings before and offered a small piece of advice which I believe made the absolute difference that day. They said, "You'll either win or you won't, so just have fun."

It was a pearl of wisdom really and it gave me clarity…I went out there feeling calm and somewhat excited. I didn't care about winning or losing, I just concentrated on golf. When something went wrong I fobbed it off. When someone else got a birdie, I didn't take any notice. When I double bogied the 14th I relaxed even more because I thought it was over and I decided to just enjoy the last few holes.

Then I noticed my partners were getting angry and frustrated at the smallest things. They were under immense pressure and it was impacting on them and they were making mistakes. The opposite was true for me.

On 17 I hit a poor tee shot on the 400-meter par 4 and managed to smack a recover shot just short of the green. I decided to putt from there and, after reading the line, focussed on speed and struck the ball with my putter just right. The pin was well back so it was a monster but it went in for a birdie.

On the last, a long par 3, I made the centre of the green and had a mid-length uphill putt on a severe slope. I didn't catch the putt well and the ball curled hard right leaving a 10 footer to save par. I was calm, didn't worry about the poor putt before and lined it up. It looked dead straight but I knew this green always sent the ball towards the river, so I allowed a cups' width of break. The ball fell in giving me a three, three finish and a one shot victory.

The lesson here wasn't about the physical ability to hit the ball it was about keeping the brain in gear, not letting adversity turn you into an emotional train wreck. Fobbing of the bad shots and focussing on what you wanted to do.

Having a clear mind was one major factor but

refusing to get angry was the key to that win.

Fucking golf, why bother?

I don't know what originally attracted you to this wonderful and often heartbreaking game but it's a game that constantly beckons you to come back, even when the chips are down and you're playing like a busted arse.

Maybe you play because of your friends or parents or maybe you just saw the game on TV and thought, "I can do that." Whatever the reason, you're hooked, just like me and you're always looking for the magic bullet that will give you a better game.

For most of us it's a regular weekend round in the club competition and that's about it. For others it's representing his or her club or pushing on to the professional ranks. No matter your aspirations, what you put into it will define what you get out of it and that includes emotional control.

Now, I'm not going to dictate to you the need to get lessons and practice, that's been said in many books over many years BUT if you don't want to do the extra work to make yourself better WHY are you getting so upset when you mess up on the course?

If someone asked you to play a musical instrument that you'd never touched before you certainly wouldn't expect perfection right? You'd take the time to learn, build experience, making lots of mistakes along the way and eventually reach some level of competency. Learning to play golf is exactly the same and just as technically complex...so why expect you're going to hit every shot with immaculate precision on the golf course? It's impossible.

Of course some will do it better than others and a rare few will be total naturals and learn without a single lesson but they are very rare birds indeed. For most of us it is hard work, so if you plan to continue hacking every Saturday without even recognising the local pro when he walks past, then you have to accept the enviable...you will stuff up fairly often. Accepting that is your first lesson.

I'm not saying you should expect to be shit at this game. Negative thoughts are destructive when it comes to golf but you have to be realistic about your ability. How good are you? I mean really...how good?

Most people measure themselves against their very best round or their very best shots and play every game with that as the benchmark of their abilities. That's so unfair. Why do that to yourself? Not even the world number 1 can play to the best of his or her ability every round. It's just not something humans can do.

If you're best ever score was a 79 on a warm day with no wind and you front up the next weekend and it's raining with a strong head wind on half the holes, then expecting to shoot 79 again is going to see you walk off with a load of anguish and yet you do expect to do it again with ease.

You need to be honest with yourself about how good a golfer you really are. What's your average score? If your best is 79 but your average is 87, then shooting 90 or 95 isn't a shocker. There's no point at all in getting down on yourself about what you perceive to be a bad score. You will hit crappy shots and rack up shitty scores and have a lot of back luck. Suck it up and give yourself some wiggle room.

Even on your very worst day, keeping your temper in check will see you walk off with a better score than the one you will shoot by allowing a brain snap or two to demolish the round completely.

Don't get me wrong, it's one of the hardest things to do, because we all set very high benchmarks by default, but getting your mind in the right place and keeping it there will see you shoot lower scores and that's without taking lessons or going to the practice fairway.

There will be good days and bad days and occasionally you'll want to hang up the clubs and never play again. For most of us it's a fleeting thought but I do know a few who have simply given up because they couldn't cope with playing poorly and feeling like shit after every round.

I'm the first to admit that terrible rounds don't feel at all good. You walk off defeated and you can't blame an opponent's good defensive move or the miraculous bomb that landed just right to see you defeated. Golf is a solo game so it all falls on you, hence the frustration we're all very much aware of.

We're also faced with factors that seem to gang up on us time and time again like luck. It can go both ways but it always seems to go against you more often than working in your favour. Rub of the green is a term you've probably heard; the way the course can dish out some elements that make you think the Universe hates your guts, like the perfect drive that finds itself in a divot or the ball hitting something invisible and flying hard right into the water or the perfect chip that doesn't stop and rolls off the back of the green or...well I don't think I need to go on, we all have many such stories and some bizarre ones too.

The interesting part is that we blame ourselves when we have bad luck. Comments like, "Well you hit it there mate" always seem to pop up when you complain. It's true, you did hit it there but you probably didn't plan for the ball to hit the edge of a sprinkler head, cannon 45 degrees to the right and stop on the butt of a tree. Its sheer bad luck and you can't do a thing about it…so I ask you, why get the shits and have a conniption when you find the ball? Ok, let a little air out in frustration but don't let it define the rest of your round.

Watch the best players in the World and you'll see that they make a lot of mistakes and have their share of bad bounces too but it's the players that deal with it best that come away with the results. That may not necessarily be a win but it may be worth thousands of dollars, securing a tour card or qualifying for a major. Often it's not about winning the match, it's about getting past your shortcomings.

Golf is going to dish up some heavy crap sometimes, that's a given; you just have to find something inside you that says "So what," and get on with it.

What kind are you?

Different people have different tendencies on the golf course when it comes to dealing with "issues" and having a tanty or two isn't uncommon. For some it's chronic.

So, what's your issue?

I'll try and work through some scenarios that might help you understand where you sit in the scheme of things. Of course it goes without saying, when we get to the solutions it's all totally up to you. I can pitch ideas and concepts all day long but if you decide, "Nah" then there's not much I can say. You have to agree you have a problem before you can do something about it.

Right then, down to tin tacks…Do you "blow up" on the course? Do you swear at every bad shot or are you a slow burner?

Some people seemingly take all the shit that's metered out to them by the Golfing Goddess without batting an eyelid. It's an enviable trait to be able to take every kick or punch that dogs the average golfer and walk off stone cold. It's also rare. The truth is they're more likely seething on the inside and their thoughts are as destructive as those who break clubs or call their mother bad names.

Let's break it down then.

Perhaps you're the kind of person who loads up on the first tee, smashes it out of bounds or into a tree and your round is over. You can't let the bad start go and it impacts on the rest of your round. You're constantly on the back foot and never focussed or able to drag it out of the mire...well nearly never. Some days that bad shot has minimal impact and you pick yourself up...but not often.

Then there are those that get through a few holes and are playing reasonably well when they suddenly whale one into the drink. They lose their temper and the rest of the day is toast.

Perhaps you slowly build up to the fall. The first bad shot or bad bounce irritates you but you wear it. The next makes you grit your teeth a bit more and then another stuff-up leads to an outburst. You fall a few shots behind when the next problem transpires and you suddenly lose concentration and F-bombs fly in all directions. The last few holes are a blur as you implode and the game is gone.

There's also that day when you tear the course apart over the first 9 holes only to collapse at the prospect of a great score. You get tense, hit a few shockers, lose a few shots to the field and finally erupt and that great game is no more than a series of "what ifs" and "could have beens."

There are other factors that can kill a round of golf too and they might not be on the golf course. Perhaps you're having a difficult time at work or there are family issue in your life. Maybe the marriage is on the rocks or the kids are sick. These can all be hidden emotions that erupt on the golf course.

I can tell you first hand that those kinds of things can dwell inside and you think you're ok but then you play golf and all Hell breaks loose.

Case in point was a time when my in-laws were

both quite ill and we were travelling to see them regularly while the doctors did everything they could. It was a harrowing time and hard on us all emotionally but my wife's folks asked that we keep living our lives and do what we loved doing. They didn't want what they were going through to stop normality, so I played golf on those weekends we didn't go to the hospital. It was a disaster. During the week I coped or dealt with the latest medical update or consoled my wife or talked to my kids about what was happening to their grandparents, all the while feeling it in the pit of my stomach, the constant pressure of their individual cancers that would ultimately take them both from us 14 months apart.

When I played golf, the emotion vented like a volcanic eruption. What was really odd is that I didn't put the two things together, not for a very long time. I simply couldn't understand that my bad golf was purely the result of my off course emotional state. I was shedding emotion on the course while they were sick and while in mourning after they passed and simply couldn't focus on the game. I shouldn't have played at all but my in-laws wanted us to keep living, so I did as they asked. I just didn't anticipate the emotional wipe-out.

Years later a friend lost a close family member and I played with him a few weeks after. He had a shocking round and his outbursts were so uncharacteristic. He swore, which I'd never heard from him before and he constantly ridiculed himself. The next week, same thing.

I sat with him after that round and said "I know what's wrong" and when I explained that it wasn't his swing that was letting him down but his off course emotional state his face changed like a revelation had been made. He, like me, didn't even connect the two situations. Once he accepted that his life off the course was escaping during the game it made sense to him and he got on with it. He knew why he was getting upset and the outbursts stopped. He didn't immediately start playing well again, too much damage had been done, but in time he got it back.

So consider the possibility that something not remotely related to golf might be affecting you on the course. It may just be that your personal "situation" at home or at work is the sole reason for some uncharacteristic outbursts. Accept it and you will start to recover your game...in time.

One more lesson here. While I was blowing my stack during that dark time, it cost me a golfing friendship. One of my regular partners started playing in other groups and finally stopped playing with me all together. I didn't get it at the time but looking back I know he was offended by my behaviour. He didn't know why I was so angry and destructive (I broke at least two clubs in that time), he just saw me as an arsehole and he didn't want to pay with me anymore. Be warned, your behaviour can have serious ramifications that you simply won't anticipate but consider it you must.

If you recognise any of the traits I've described, and I've simply scratched the surface here, then it's not all over...but right now...I mean right this minute you should ask yourself if you want to change. Do you want to beat back the demons and not succumb to the anger, whatever the cause?

Take some time to think about a recent outburst. Why did it happen? Was it really worth reacting that way? What impact did it have on your game, your emotional state or your playing partners? Think about it and make a pact with yourself to change.

Dealing with the crap

Ok, so here we are at the business end of the book. I told you it was a short read because it really isn't a major psychological problem you're dealing with, it's simply an over-reaction to a meaningless situation that no-one else gives a shit about...am I right?

Think about this, you're playing with your regular group and the shit hits the fan, you lose your marbles and let loose on God or Jesus or some other deity while your friends look on. They might be amused; they might be tolerant or it might be the last straw. The fact is you're comfortable doing your block with them because you've been playing together for a long time. What if a woman joined the group one day and you played badly and started feeling the anger well up, would you blow your top then? I think not.

There are some that say anger isn't normal, that it isn't a natural manifestation of our being. In short, we choose to get angry. That's why, when you're playing with new people you might curb those tendencies and perhaps vent with mild frustration or a grunt. It proves that you can control yourself if you have to. AND I'll bet you played better too, and even if you didn't, I'll bet you walked off feeling better than on those days when you let your brain's gearbox slip into neutral and red line the tacometer!

If you agree with me on this point, then you have to agree that there's really never a situation that requires you to "go off" when your game goes south. Choose to accept the good, the bad and the downright hideous elements of golf because you'll soon realise it can offer you some good things too. You might start to have fun, get some great bounces, be acknowledge for playing a good shot, be seen as someone who is nice to play with, make new friends and, most importantly, enjoy yourself regularly. Who knows...but being a bombastic dickhead isn't going to give you any of that.

OK, let's say your handicap is 11. You probably expect to shoot around 82 or 83 depending on the course par, slope rating etc. right? Why put that much pressure on yourself? Give yourself some space to relax. Set yourself a target of say 87. You'll seriously surprise yourself when you play a more relaxed game because you haven't put too much pressure on yourself to shoot super low. You'll probably beat 87 most times and end up with a number of sub 80 rounds. In short, size up your handicap index and give yourself a few extra shots, just to take the heat off...it will work wonders.

For some, keeping statistics will maintain focus. Even on a bad day you know you can run up some good number statistically. You may have a terrible driving day but only have 29 putts. Keeping track of your Average score, Fairways hit, Greens in regulation, up and down percentages, Sand save, Putts per round or any number of variables will almost always give you a positive. It may also reveal a part of the game that is letting you down and you can work on it if you like to practice. Keep the data on a spreadsheet or use one of the many stats web sites that are available. You may keep your cool just knowing that you're improving a certain statistic. Don't write it down as you play, that's distracting...reflect on it after the game. I often reviewed rounds while taking a shower and often put a bad round to only one or two holes, which really isn't a big deal.

I don't believe in the claim that holding your breath and counting to ten will suddenly wipe away the anger but there are things you can do. I once kept a golf diary and wrote my thoughts down after each round, whether I played well or not. I dragged it out the other day and thumbed through some of the pages. I was surprised by how many nice things I said about myself. Even on the days where I shot horrible scores, I found something good to write down..." Shot 92 today, shocking score but it was a medal round and the course was very wet after two days of rain. Most of the field had the same problem so it wasn't as bad as it looked" or "Was five down after four holes today. I fought back to finish two down. Very proud of how I kept it together".

You can also learn from the good rounds too, "Had a blinder today. Really played well and didn't let the bad shots bother me at all. I rejected all my bad thoughts too. Good job."

This approach might not be for you but positive reinforcement goes a long way towards reprogramming your mind. You have to accept you can change and talking yourself into it is going to go a long way towards getting there. Writing it down and referring to it from time to time will make you a more positive player. Believe me it works.

Another tool you can use is positive affirmation. Lots of Pros take this approach, just a few lines written on a piece of paper that they read out load to themselves every day, "I am a great golfer. I am always focussed. I am happiest when I play golf. I enjoy playing every game."

You can make up your own and you'll find

hundreds of them on the Internet and be able to tailor them to suit yourself. Give it a try.

Another thing to try is talking yourself to sleep at night by saying positive things about your game. Just keep repeating those affirmations in your mind until you drop off. You go to sleep with positive programming.

Now this is probably going to sound lame but if you're not into taking diary notes or self-talk then perhaps you have the strength of mind to simply stop getting angry with yourself. I mean it. Before your next round simply agree that you won't lose your crap on the course and make a determined effort to reject the anger. Then, next time you play, do it again...and again. In time it will just be normal. Sure you'll have the occasional relapse, but like any habit you're trying to break, you have to keep at it before you totally succeed. It's just possible that saying "no" to getting angry will work in your case.

While you're at it, try rejecting negative thoughts. Instead of seeing the ball flying into the water, shake your head and say "no" to yourself and reject the idea of it. Just simply refuse to accept the thought. Actually say it to yourself under your breath, "No!"

What about fear? Are you scared of stuffing up, do you fear failure or even fear success while you play? Fear leads to mistakes which creates anger. The simple solution is to confront those feelings, agree they exist and decide not to worry. Play with a plan and commitment. Better to give a shot 100% even when it turns out to be a wrong club choice or you forgot to allow for the wind. Be decisive, not scared.

I'm sure we've all been in this situation. You're playing a championship round, a medal round or an average club round and one of your partners is about as good as you in terms of skill and handicap. You want to focus on beating him but he gets off to a good start with a couple of birdies and you suddenly feel pressure to catch up but you play worse and get agitated and finally blow your stack. The issue here is that you're worrying about something you can't control. Take no notice of him or his score. Casually acknowledge his good shot or good putt but don't dwell on it... just play your game. Chances are he'll have a bad hole or two later. Perhaps your good play will sway him...who knows?

OK, I have a confession to make and I don't do this lightly but I was playing so poorly at one stage that my wife bought me a session with a hypnotist. I was so desperate for help I decided it couldn't hurt to give it a try. Of course, this isn't for everyone and I'm still not sure how it worked but for the next two games I was runner up and got a hole in one. I kid you not! But like all good things, it wore off. I'm not sure if I was actually hypnotically tranced into playing better or was somehow living the illusion that my problems were over but for a few weeks I believed and because I had a completely new mind set, good things happened.

You can also try chatting about anything other than golf between shots. Just talk to your partners about news, politics or tell bad jokes. It's remarkably calming.

Stop calling yourself an idiot, or a moron or any number of self-deprecating and insulting names after striking a poor shot. A short and sweet point I know but quite valid. Just don't do it.

It's possible that none of these ideas will work for you, or you might think of other ways to curb your tendencies, but reading this book says one thing to me, you know you have a problem and you want to do something about it. If I've missed the mark with you, don't give up...search for another way. It's worth it.

Some final thoughts

Let me finish by offering some recommended reading. If you're deadly serious about improving your mind and thinking strategically then you need to rewire your brain and who better than some experts in the field...and they're not paying me to say this. They don't even know I exist. I simply bought these books to learn more about thinking on the golf course and hoped they would help me...and they did. It also sparked my journalistic interest and prompted me to do a lot of research into the nonphysical side of golf and I have to say it was enlightening.

One of the best in the golfing mind business has to be Dr. Bob Rotella. He's written multiple books on various aspects of the game and worked with some of the top pros on the PGA

Tour. Any of his books would be worth reading, but the one that stood out was "The Golfer's Mind" a truly excellent book in my opinion and a watershed moment in my golfing life.

Bob's other books are all excellent, "Golf is a Game of Confidence", "Golf is Not a Game of Perfect", "The Golf of Your Dreams" and "Putting Out of Your Mind".

Another book worth considering is "8 Traits of the Champion Golfer" by Deborah Graham and John Stabler. This was the first book I bought about retraining the mind when it comes to golf and really got me wanting to know so much more.

"Zen Golf" and "How to Make Every Putt" by Dr. Joseph Parent are both very good reads as well.

These books delve into the mind very deeply and look at how to think around the course, what to focus on and how to stay in the moment. And there are many more if you want to look for them.

I hope my short book has given you some insight into the ability to beat off your demons and fight the anger that has become such a habit in your game and indeed your life. It doesn't have to be that way but you are the only one who can change it and make the decisions that will set you on the right path.

You have to be committed and you have to stick to you guns because, as I said at the start, if you don't keep on top of the anger it will consume you again and you may, like me, find it much harder to beat the second time around.

Be positive, believe in yourself and fight off those demons. You have to accept that it might be a slow journey, it might not be easy and there may be relapses and days of downright failure but if you persist and focus, then anger and frustration certainly are beatable and you'll be a much better player for it.

Good luck and don't forget to like yourself.

Andrew Dunkley

© Copyright 2016

Lightning Source UK Ltd.
Milton Keynes UK
UKHW010619311219
356163UK00001B/114/P